The Great Pyramid

Egypt's Tomb for All Time

By Jeanette Leardi

Consultant: Dr. Phyllis Saretta
Egyptologist and Lecturer
The Metropolitan Museum of Art

BEARPORT
PUBLISHING

New York, New York

Credits

Cover and title page, © M. Timothy O'Keefe; 4, © M. Timothy O'Keefe / Alamy; 5, © Andrea Jemolo / akg-images; 7, © Mary Jelliffe / Ancient Art & Architecture Collection Ltd; 8L, © ARPL / HIP / The Image Works; 8R, © Ronald Sheridan / Ancient Art & Architecture Collection; 9T, © HIP / Art Resource, NY; 9B, © Réunion des Musées Nationaux / Art Resource, NY; 10, © Gordana Uzelac / agefotostock.com; 12, © Digital Globe / AP Images; 13T, © The Art Archive / Egyptian Museum Cairo / Dagli Orti; 13B, © Werner Forman / Art Resource, NY; 14, © Ronald Sheridan / Ancient Art & Architecture Collection Ltd; 15, © SSPL / The Image Works; 16, © Paul Almasy/CORBIS; 17, © AFP PHOTO/HO/MENA/Newscom.com; 18, © Hervé Champollion / akg-images; 19, © John P. Stevens / Ancient Art & Architecture Collection Ltd; 20, © Tor Eigeland / Alamy; 21T, © Erich Lessing / Art Resource, NY; 21B, © Kenneth Garrett/National Geographic/ Getty Images; 22, © Samantha Lee/Ovoworks/Ovoworks/Time Life Pictures/Getty Images; 23, © LL/Roger Viollet/Getty Images; 24, © Kenneth Garrett / National Geographic; 25, © Reuters/ CORBIS; 26, © INFOCUS Photos / Alamy; 27, Graham White; 29, © MARWAN NAAMANI/ AFP/Getty Images.

Publisher: Kenn Goin
Project Editor: Adam Siegel
Creative Director: Spencer Brinker
Original Design: Dawn Beard Creative and Triesta Hall of Blu-Design

Library of Congress Cataloging-in-Publication Data

Leardi, Jeanette.
  The Great Pyramid : Egypt's tomb for all time / by Jeanette Leardi.
    p. cm. — (Castles, palaces & tombs)
  Includes bibliographical references and index.
  ISBN-13: 978-1-59716-266-1 (library binding)
  ISBN-10: 1-59716-266-3 (library binding)
  ISBN-13: 978-1-59716-294-4 (pbk.)
  ISBN-10: 1-59716-294-9 (pbk.)
 1. Great Pyramid (Egypt)—Juvenile literature. I. Title. II. Series.

  DT63.L39 2007
  932—dc22
                    2006005857

For more information, write to Bearport Publishing Company, Inc., 101 Fifth Avenue, Suite 6R, New York, New York 10003. Printed in the United States of America.

10 9 8 7 6 5 4 3 2 1

Table of Contents

Thousands at Work 4

Who Were the Pharaohs? 6

Making Mummies 8

A Towering Tomb 10

Guiding Lights 12

How Did They Do It? 14

Who Built the Great Pyramid? 16

A Peek Inside 18

Three Pyramids for Three Pharaohs 20

Guardian of the Tombs 22

Still Digging for Facts 24

Visiting the Great Pyramid 26

Just the Facts 28

Timeline 29

Glossary 30

Bibliography 31

Read More 31

Learn More Online 31

Index 32

About the Author 32

Thousands at Work

In the sun's blazing heat, a group of Egyptians arrived at a desert along the banks of the Nile River. They had traveled hundreds of miles by boat. They were scared, but excited. Never before had they left their tiny villages.

The Great Pyramid was built about 4,600 years ago in Egypt near the town of Giza.

As the Egyptians stepped off the boat, they saw 20,000 workers. Many were cutting giant blocks of limestone. Others were pulling huge stones up the slanted sides of a building. All had come at the **command** of their king, Khufu (KOO-foo). They were doing the most important work of their lives. They were building Khufu's **tomb**—the Great Pyramid.

Khufu ruled Egypt from about 2551 to 2528 B.C. This small statue, about 3 inches (8 cm) tall, is the only record of what he looked like.

Who Were the Pharaohs?

Who was this king who could order such a mighty task? He was an ancient Egyptian ruler, called **pharaoh**. Yet to the Egyptian people, their king was not just a powerful man. He was the sky god, Horus (HOR-us), who had come down to Earth.

Today, Cairo is the capital of Egypt. In Khufu's time, Memphis was the capital, which is 11 miles (18 km) south of Cairo.

The pharaoh was all-powerful. His word was law. Everyone paid **taxes** to the pharaoh. Many Egyptians used crops or animals to pay taxes. They also paid by working for the ruler. They built his palaces—and his tomb.

Painting of pharaoh Ramesses III

The pharaohs ruled over ancient Egypt for thousands of years, beginning around 3000 B.C.

Making Mummies

A pharaoh's death marked the end of his time on Earth. Now he could continue his life among the gods. The Egyptians believed the pharaoh needed his body to enjoy this **afterlife**. So they **preserved** his body as a **mummy**.

Prayers were written on a mummy's case to guide and protect the person in the afterlife.

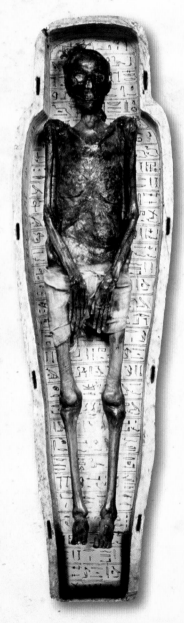

An unwrapped Egyptian mummy

First, the body was washed. The pharoah's insides, such as the lungs and stomach, were put in jars. The brain was thrown away. The pharaoh's heart, however, was left in place. Egyptians believed the heart was where thoughts and feelings came from. The body was then dried with salt and wrapped in cloth. Finally, it was put in a **coffin**.

Each of these jars held a different part of the mummy's body. From left to right, the jars held the person's lungs, stomach, intestines, and liver.

Crocodile mummies

Sacred animals such as cats, crocodiles, and birds were also mummified.

A Towering Tomb

Like other pharaohs before him, Khufu ordered workers to build him a tomb. It would hold his body and his treasures. So he wanted the building to be strong enough to last forever. Yet Khufu wanted something more. He wanted his tomb to be the tallest one ever built—and it was. Khufu's pyramid stood 481 feet (147 m) tall.

There are more than 100 pyramids in Egypt. Almost all of them were built to be used as tombs.

This is the first pyramid built in Egypt, more than 4,600 years ago. Unlike later pyramids, its sides were not smooth, but looked like steps.

Building the Great Pyramid took lots of planning. The tomb would need tightly closed rooms to keep out robbers. It would also need **air shafts**. These airways may have been built to help Khufu's spirit travel to the heavens.

An Inside View of the Great Pyramid

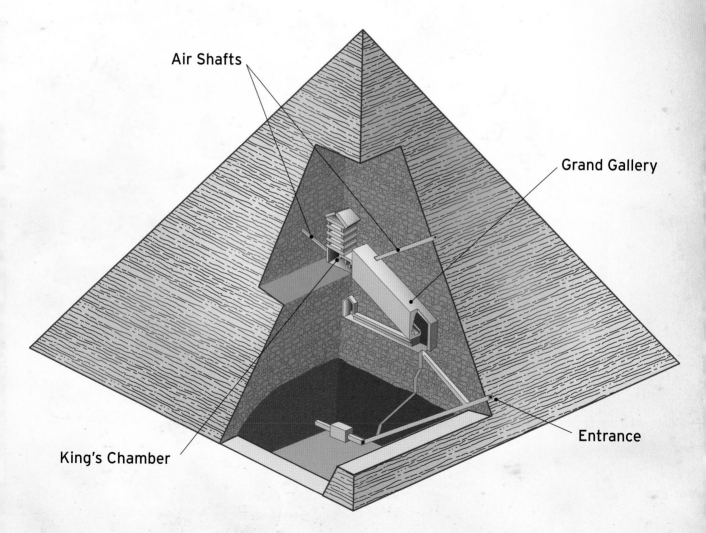

Air Shafts

Grand Gallery

Entrance

King's Chamber

Khufu's mummy was placed in a room called the King's Chamber.

Guiding Lights

The sun and stars played an important role in Egyptian religion. These lights in the sky may have also been used in choosing the shape and location of the Great Pyramid.

The sides of the tomb were sloped. This slanted shape may have stood for the sun's slanting rays. Some **historians** believe that the Egyptians thought the sun's rays would guide the pharaoh's spirit to the afterlife.

The Great Pyramid from above

The Great Pyramid's walls were built so that each one faced a different direction— north, south, east, and west.

12

The Egyptians believed that certain groups of stars, or **constellations**, were sacred. These stars would also guide Khufu's spirit. So the builders lined up the pyramid's walls and air shafts to face them.

This painting shows the Egyptian belief that the journey to the afterlife was made in a boat.

In 1954, Khufu's ship was found next to the Great Pyramid. It is believed that Egyptians buried it near Khufu's tomb so that the ship could help carry him into the afterlife.

How Did They Do It?

Once it was decided where the pyramid's walls would lie, the building could begin. Workers cut huge stones from rock **quarries**. They did this using simple hand tools. Some stones were sent to Giza by boat on the Nile River. Others were dragged to the **site** using ropes and wooden sleds.

This wall painting shows how workers used a sled to pull blocks of stone.

No one knows how the workers got the stones to the top of the pyramid. Most stones weighed about 2.5 tons (2.3 metric tons). The builders may have used one big **ramp**. Or they may have built a ramp that wrapped around the pyramid. In all, it took more than two million stones to complete the pyramid.

Workers used simple tools to cut the pyramid stones, such as this chisel (top) and sharpening stone (bottom).

It took about 20 years to build the Great Pyramid. Some **archaeologists** say that the workers must have put one stone in place about every two minutes.

15

Who Built the Great Pyramid?

Workers came to Giza from every part of Egypt to help build Khufu's tomb. About 5,000 **skilled** workers stayed there throughout the year. Many were artists and stonecutters. About 20,000 others worked for three to four months each year. They did the hard tasks of dragging the stones.

From about July to October, the Nile River flooded the land around it. Most of the work on the Great Pyramid was done during these months, when people couldn't farm their land.

Archaeologists once believed that slaves built the Great Pyramid. Now they know that the workers were free Egyptians. Bread and beer were used to pay them. The workers had their own city by the Great Pyramid. They believed that by building their pharaoh's tomb, they would have a better afterlife, too.

The workers' city near the Great Pyramid had bakeries, houses, butcher shops, and even cemeteries. The outlines of the buildings' walls can still be seen today.

A Peek Inside

The outside of the Great Pyramid is amazing to see. Yet the inside is just as wonderful. A long, narrow hallway with a high ceiling leads to the King's Chamber. The stones inside the King's Chamber fit together very tightly. Even a playing card cannot fit between them.

This long hallway is called the Grand Gallery. It leads to the King's Chamber, where Khufu's mummy was placed.

Khufu's mummy was put in a great stone case in the King's Chamber. Today, only the stone case remains in the room. How do archaeologists know that this was Khufu's tomb? In smaller rooms above the chamber, workers wrote Khufu's name using pictures, called **hieroglyphs**.

This is all that remains of the stone case, called a sarcophagus (sar-KAHF-uh-gus), in which Khufu's mummy lay.

Khufu's name written in hieroglyphs

Despite careful planning, robbers broke into the Great Pyramid. They stole Khufu's mummy. No one knows exactly when this happened. Khufu's mummy has never been found.

Three Pyramids for Three Pharaohs

Khufu's tomb was the pride of Egypt. At the time, no building in the world was larger. Yet Khufu's son, the pharaoh Khafre (KAHF-ray), wanted his own tomb to be even greater. He built his pyramid next to his father's, but on higher ground. It looks taller. Yet it's actually shorter by 8 feet (2 m).

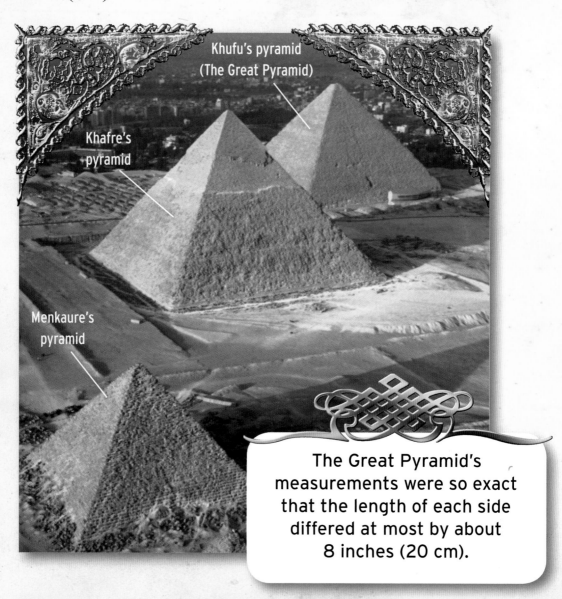

Khufu's pyramid
(The Great Pyramid)

Khafre's pyramid

Menkaure's pyramid

The Great Pyramid's measurements were so exact that the length of each side differed at most by about 8 inches (20 cm).

Khafre's son, the pharaoh Menkaure (men-KOW-ray), built a smaller pyramid for himself. Besides these three pyramids, several very small ones were built for the Egyptian queens. Also at the Giza site are several **temples**. These were places where people offered food to the pharaohs' spirits and to the gods.

The pharaoh Khafre

The pharaoh Menkaure

Guardian of the Tombs

In front of Khafre's pyramid is one of the most famous statues in the world. It has the head of a man and the body of a lion. It is called the Sphinx (SFINKS).

The Sphinx is a statue of the sun god at dawn. For this reason, it faces the east—the direction where the sun rises.

Many archaeologists believe that Khafre ordered the Sphinx's face to be carved to look like his own.

Most of the Sphinx was carved from one huge block of limestone. It was made to guard the pyramids from enemies. Time has worn away much of the statue. Yet it is still a mighty sight to see.

The Sphinx around 1865

During much of its life, wind-blown sand covered the Sphinx up to its neck. The statue was completely uncovered around 1926.

Still Digging for Facts

Today, the Great Pyramid still holds secrets. Archaeologists keep looking for answers about how it was built. They continue to discover many things. In the 1990s, they found large mud pots used for baking bread. In 2005, six new rooms were found near the Great Pyramid. In these rooms were 404 small statues.

An archaeologist holds a bread mold that was found along with plates and a dough-mixing pot near the Great Pyramid.

Archaeologists have had to find new ways of looking inside the Great Pyramid. The air shafts are too small for a person to crawl through. So they built a robot that could easily move through them. Only time, and more searching, will tell what other secrets lie within the tomb.

This robot, the Pyramid Rover, has a camera that shows what it sees inside the air shafts.

Archaeologists have found the names of some of the Great Pyramid's workers on the inside walls. They believe this shows that the builders were proud of their work.

Visiting the Great Pyramid

Visitors to the Giza pyramids can walk around the site. They also can go inside the pyramids and buildings that are open that day. At night there is a sound and light show. It tells about the history of the Giza pyramids.

The Great Pyramid during the sound and light show

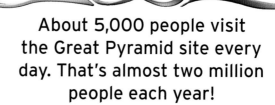

About 5,000 people visit the Great Pyramid site every day. That's almost two million people each year!

The pyramids have lasted for thousands of years. Yet these tombs need to be protected. Air **pollution** can hurt the stone. So cars and buses are not allowed near the buildings. Security cameras make sure no one writes or carves on the stone walls. With care, the Great Pyramid will remain what it was meant to be: Egypt's tomb for all time.

The Pyramids of Giza

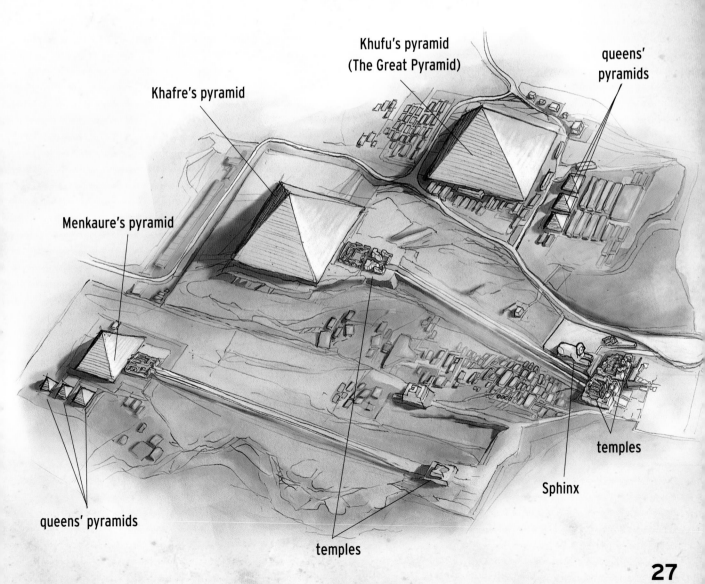

Khufu's pyramid
(The Great Pyramid)

queens' pyramids

Khafre's pyramid

Menkaure's pyramid

temples

Sphinx

queens' pyramids

temples

Just the Facts

- The Great Pyramid is one of the Seven Wonders of the Ancient World, and the only one still standing today.

- At 481 feet (147 m), the Great Pyramid was the tallest building in the world for more than 3,000 years.

- Many of the stones that formed the Great Pyramid's outer shell were later taken away to build houses and other buildings in nearby Cairo.

- The word *pharaoh* means "great house." The word was first used to describe the royal palace, not the king.

- The very top of the Great Pyramid is missing. Some archaeologists think it may have been made of gold.

- The French general Napoleon estimated that all the stones used in the three pyramids could build a wall around France that would be 10 feet (3 m) high and 1 foot (0.3 m) thick.

Timeline

No one knows exactly when Khufu, Khafre, and Menkaure ruled, or when the Great Pyramid was built. Here is one possible timeline.

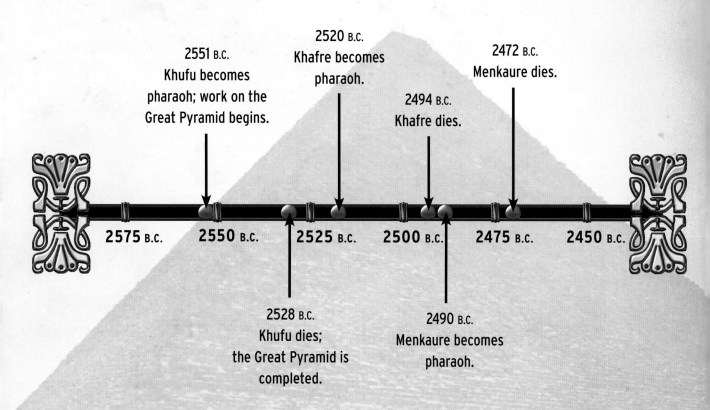

2551 B.C.
Khufu becomes pharaoh; work on the Great Pyramid begins.

2520 B.C.
Khafre becomes pharaoh.

2494 B.C.
Khafre dies.

2472 B.C.
Menkaure dies.

2575 B.C.   2550 B.C.   2525 B.C.   2500 B.C.   2475 B.C.   2450 B.C.

2528 B.C.
Khufu dies; the Great Pyramid is completed.

2490 B.C.
Menkaure becomes pharaoh.

Glossary

afterlife (AF-tur-*life*) the life a person has after he or she dies

air shafts (AIR SHAFTS) small tunnels that let air through

archaeologists (*ar*-kee-OL-uh-jists) scientists who learn about ancient times by studying things they dig up, such as old buildings, tools, and pottery

coffin (KAWF-in) a container in which a dead person is placed for burying

command (kuh-MAND) an order, usually given by a ruler or someone else in charge

constellations (*kon*-stuh-LAY-shunz) groups of stars that form a shape in the night sky

hieroglyphs (HYE-ur-uh-*glifs*) pictures used in ancient Egyptian writing

historians (hi-STOR-ee-uhnz) people who study the past

mummy (MUH-mee) the preserved body of a dead person or animal

pharaoh (FAIR-oh) ruler of ancient Egypt

pollution (puh-LOO-shuhn) anything that makes something unhealthy or dirty

preserved (pri-ZURVD) kept in good condition

quarries (KWOR-eez) places in the ground or along the sides of hills where large rocks are cut

ramp (RAMP) a slope used to roll, push, or pull something up or down

sacred (SAY-krid) holy, religious

site (SITE) a place where a building is being built or already stands

skilled (SKILD) having a special talent or ability

taxes (TAKS-iz) money people pay to support the government

temples (TEM-puhlz) religious buildings where people worship

tomb (TOOM) a grave, room, or building in which a dead body is buried

Bibliography

Morell, Virginia. "The Pyramid Builders." *National Geographic* (November 2001), pp. 78–99.

Silverman, David P., ed. *Ancient Egypt.* New York: Oxford University Press (1997).

Smith, Craig B. *How the Great Pyramid Was Built.* Washington, D.C.: Smithsonian Books (2004).

Verner, Miroslav. *The Pyramids: The Mystery, Culture, and Science of Egypt's Great Monuments.* New York: Grove Press (2001).

http://guardians.net/hawass

www.bbc.co.uk/history/ancient/egyptians

www.pbs.org/wgbh/nova/pyramid

Read More

Bingham, Caroline. *DK Eye Wonder: Pyramid.* New York: DK Publishing, Inc. (2004).

Chrisp, Peter. *Ancient Egypt Revealed.* New York: DK Publishing, Inc. (2002).

Macaulay, David. *Pyramid.* Boston, MA: Houghton Mifflin/Walter Lorraine Books (1975).

Millard, Anne. *Mysteries of the Pyramids.* Brookfield, CT: Copper Beech Books (1995).

Nardo, Don. *Daily Life: Ancient Egypt.* San Diego, CA: KidHaven Press (2002).

Learn More Online

Visit these Web sites to learn more about pyramids and ancient Egypt:

www.ancientegypt.co.uk/pyramids

www.nationalgeographic.com/pyramids

Index

afterlife 8, 12–13, 17
air pollution 27
air shafts 11, 13, 25
archaeologists 15, 17, 19, 22,
    24–25, 28

Cairo 6, 28
constellations 13

Giza 4, 6, 14, 16, 21, 26–27
Grand Gallery 11, 18

hieroglyphs 19
Horus 6

Khafre 20–21, 22, 27, 29
Khufu 5, 6, 10–11, 13, 16, 18–19,
    20, 27, 29
Khufu's ship 13
King's Chamber 11, 18–19

Memphis 6
Menkaure 20–21, 27, 29
mummy 8–9, 11, 18–19

Napoleon 28
Nile River 4, 6, 14, 16

pharaoh 6–7, 8–9, 10, 12, 17,
    20–21, 28–29

queens 21, 27

robbers 11, 19
robot 25

sarcophagus 19
sound and light show 26
Sphinx 22–23, 27

taxes 7
temples 21, 27
tomb 5, 7, 10–11, 12–13, 16–17,
    19, 20, 22, 25, 27

workers 5, 7, 10, 14–15, 16–17,
    19, 25

About the Author

Jeanette Leardi is a freelance writer and editor in
Charlotte, North Carolina. She has written many educational
books for children, and poems, articles, and essays for adults.